THEY WOULD NOT BE

Poems by

TOM T. HALL

Peggy,
love ya!!
Tom T.

© 2017 by Good Home Grown Books

Dedications

This book is dedicated to two ladies who have played a part in my literary efforts over the years.

Judi Marshall managed my office and all of my activities for thirty-five years. She was the first to read and work on all of my books, including this one. She was part of my family and celebrated and sorrowed with us through the good and bad times. More good than bad. I was going to say how much I love her, but she already knows.

Sue McClure. Sometimes copy editor, longtime friend, and one of the great platonic loves of my life. Thanks Sue for copy editing this book.

Contents

Preface

It is the way of the world that old men think they have learned something that needs sharing.

Songwriters spend their days musing on bits and pieces of information, inspiration and all manner of intellectual trivia. It seems unfair to leave a few less-than perfect tomatoes in the garden. And so I leave you with this bowl of scraps from the soil I have tilled and pillaged for so long.

These are things that will not leave my memory. They want to be something and I could find no melody or meter for them. What's to be done?

For better or worse, I give them this little life of their own.

The Invisible Zero

When I was a boy of seven
I stood at the edge of the schoolyard
Hands clasped behind my back
I stared off into the sky
The teacher tapped me on the shoulder
You're always doing this
Staring off into space
Go play with the other children
We worry about you
What are you doing
I said I could imagine nothing
I could close my eyes and make everything go away
Everything
The sky
The world
And me too
Nothing
Now she was in front of me
She looked frightened
Promise me you'll stop doing that
Go play with the other children
I said I would stop doing it
I kept my word and never did
I am an old man now
Afraid to try it
I have two fears
One is that I couldn't do it
The other is that I could

Inanimate Love

I have loved two inanimate objects in my life
One a bulldozer
And the other a guitar
With the bulldozer the earth moved
And likewise with the guitar
And made me who I am

I'll Say This

There is something about name-dropping
Something sticky
Like looking for a light switch in the dark
I'll say this
I have known some famous poets
Most of them taught poetry
Training up competition
Like loading a gun
Anticipating suicide
I'll say this
Some poets will be left
When you are gone

Joyce Kilmer And Me And Trees

Joyce Kilmer wrote:

.....poems are made by fools like me
but only God can make a tree

I wrote:

H
E
R
E
AT LAST
FOR ALL TO SEE
A POEM EXACTLY LIKE A
T
R
E
E

A Hard Place and A Rock

Despite what the Indians say
There was no good day to die
So he picked a Friday
He was a stone mason
Rock entrances to gated communities
Maple Acres starting at $350,000
He ended it with one of his rock walls
Police say he was doing ninety
Not wearing his seat belt

A Maybe Harvest

As a small country boy
I sat in the general store
Away from the wood-burning
Potbelly stove
Where sat the farmers in winter
Talking and planning spring crops
Fertilizer water weather mules and seeds
Like songwriters in Nashville
Sitting in air-conditioned writing rooms
Trying to craft the next song
Catch a break
Get a hit
Many the turn of the wheel
Before the harvest

A Trick My Dog Taught Me

I lived in the backwoods of Kentucky
I was a little boy
I had a B-B gun and a dog
We hunted
A rabbit darted into the brush
My dog darted into the brush
I darted into the brush
And grabbed a limb that stopped me
I saw my dog fall over a ten-foot cliff
He landed with a dust-flying thump
Got up
Shook himself off and kept going
He never once looked back
I thought
What a great idea
I could re-write this and make it better
But

Poets And Nature

When I go out for my morning walk
With my dog Pal
We see nature in all it's glory
I can't write words of such beauty
But Pal is a real poet
He pisses on the roses

Accepting Fate

As a teen-ager in my small home town
Population 1500
Parked in an old Ford coupe
A buddy of mine and I were drinking beer
His arm was out the window
He dropped an empty beer can
The sound rattled through the small town
Like a gunshot
The police station was a block away
Two officers emerged
They knew the illegal sound of the beer can
My buddy jumped from the car and ran
Toward the railroad tracks and the river beyond
The officers started yelling and shooting
Real bullets
I eased the car into gear and drove away
To his mother's house
I knocked on her door
The police are after Teddy
He's been drinking
They were shooting at him
She looked at me through eyes that knew sorrow
She said
Something's gonna kill us all
And closed the door

Ah So

Napping on a train from Tokyo to Osaka
One-hundred-plus miles per hour
With my interpreter and guide for my tour
I am exhausted
My aide says
Hall-san
Yes
Want some green tea
No sir thank you
He sighs
A few minutes later
Hall-san
Yes
You want something to eat
No thank you
He sighs
A few minutes later
Hall-san
Yes
You want a beer
No thank you
He sighs and says
I sure would rike to see the Brue Ridge Mountains

Negotiations

Riding on my tour bus
Sitting at the table drinking coffee
My guitar player sat down opposite
Can we talk
Sure
You pay me good and I like my job
Good
Elvis pays Jimmy Burton thirty-five hundred a week
We have two problems
How's that
I'm not Elvis and you're not Jimmy Burton

An Inconvenient Coyote

The coyote sits at the edge of my field
I suspect its instinct is keener than my supposed intelligence
Ears perked forward it stares at me
It wants my chickens
There are hungry pups back in the hollow
My chickens are penned up
Wire on the sides and top of the pen
I could turn one of my chickens loose
Leave it out for the night
It would be gone in the morning
The coyote would be back tomorrow
Ears perked forward
I live on this planet with others like me
Some are old and sick
Some are young and hungry
Some are mentally incompetent
Whatever that means
We scream on TV
No welfare!
No health care!
No taxes!
They're not my kids!
I have my chickens
The pups are hungry
I get it
I am guilty
When mankind has gone the way of the dinosaurs
What will be said of the species?
...They accumulated

Definition of Poetry

Dictionaries are cautious
About telling us what poetry means
I hereby let the cat out of the bag
Poetry is prose that has been
Boiled
Bleached
Laundered
Left out in the sun to dry
Starched
Ironed
Processed
Though the digestive system
Of a pedantic bull
And hung out on a line

As The Eagle Flies

I have forgotten who called
They had rescued a wounded eagle
It had healed
Now they would release it into the wild
They would like me to give it a name
A great American name
Several celebrities had done this
One named his Freedom
Another opted for Liberty
And so on
I thought for a moment
For some reason I cannot explain
My childhood dog came to mind
I often think of how good and loyal he was
He would be honored
I said
I would like to name my eagle Spot
I never heard from them again
Sorry Spot

Bamboo

Writers make a living with words
I think we wasted the word *Bamboo*
We gave it to a long stemmed plant
Used it for fishing poles and furniture
Writers could have made better use of *Bamboo*
Movies
Return of The Bamboo
Bamboos Gone Wild
Songs
I Wonder Where My Bamboo Is Tonight
Baby names
Bamboo Bubba Jones
Fishing poles
Really

Blood Water And Air

Blood is thicker than water
Water is thicker than air
Babies are all of these things and more
For all that we know or care
He looks like his daddy they said to me
A mystic thread runs on
Part of the joy we see in our kids
Is us even though we are gone

Brevity Barrier

I was invited to give a talk at a prestigious southern university
They even gave me the topic on which I was to speak
The topic was a question
What would you do if you had one week to live
I spent a lot of time thinking about the invitation
It took a lot of pondering and musing
Nothing ever worked
I turned it down because of the brevity of my speech
Start screaming

Science and Sanity

Spoiler alert
I do not know the answer to the question I will shortly ask
The Principal of my grade school was a member of the Flat Earth
Society
Our textbooks told us differently
I have known since then that the earth is round
As I write this I am eighty years old
In all of this time
Why have politicians learned nothing
And blood still puddles on the flat earth

Coffee Sack Annie

People in rural Kentucky called a burlap bag a coffee sack
There was an old and stooped woman we called a witch
Who carried her belongings in a coffee sack
We children were terrified of this woman
One day my uncle accidentally cut himself with an ax
My aunt turned to me
Only one person can stop bleeding
Go tell Coffee Sack Annie to stop the bleeding
And hurry
I ran into the woods and sat down under a tree
I waited until enough time had passed
I closed my eyes
Clapped my hands three times and said
Stop the bleeding
I ran back to the house
My aunt said
The bleeding has stopped
I told you so
A few years later someone said the word warlock
I said
What's a warlock
That's when it started to bother me

Dallas Airport

They used to say
Spend two days at the Dallas airport
And you will get to see
Every country entertainer currently working
So
A plane arrives from Hawaii
A big fat lady and her tiny husband deplane
The husband is loaded down with shopping bags
Cameras around his neck armloads of souvenirs
The poor little man is fifty yards down the concourse
The woman grabs me by the arm and hangs on
Herman! Herman!
The little man turns and starts struggling back
Herman! Do you know who this is
Meekly
No
This is Mel Tillis!

Demographics

It took a while for Las Vegas to figure me out

I drew big crowds

The thing they finally discovered

My fans were all broke

My fans had no money to gamble with

The folks in Vegas should have listened to my songs

Doubling Down On The Euphemism

She lost her mother
Go console her
He was a young preacher
Just out of seminary
He had never done this before
The funeral director lifted the lid
The daughter screamed
Who is that woman
Your mother
That's not my mother
Sometimes when people cross over...
That's not my mother
Sometimes when we are grieving...
Who the hell is this woman
I know my own mother
This happened a long time ago
All of these people have passed on

Einstein's Violin

Perfect phrase on violin

Never to be heard again

Time and space and gravity

Never will be two of these

Generation Gulp

When my son Dean was a little boy
We saw a beautiful black and gold sunset
I say
Lets make some cloud pictures
Okay
A few minutes pass
I say
Wow look at that train
Pause
Where
Right at the edge of that tree line
I don't see it
You can't see that big black train
Oh
I'm sorry I was making pictures out of the gold

Gentle Losers

All hail the gentle losers
You see only their backs
As they move away to their special no place

They give us in word and thought
What they could never give us in rock
The knowing and the marveling of it

One Wednesday afternoon at four
Or some such time
It becomes a part of us and important
What should we say to their backs
Thank you
No
Let it be

Graduation Day

Basic training
United States Army
I am crawling through cold mud
With an M-1 rifle
Keeping my rifle dry
Keeping my head down
Crawling over slimy logs
A sergeant steps on my helmet
Pushing my face into the mud
Shouts
Keep your head down
He laughs
I knew then that I had completed my military indoctrination
If my gun had been loaded
I would have shot the son-of-a-bitch

How Not To Get Lost In The Fifties

I took piano lessons as a child
Learned scales
All musical instruments have them
For each key
Whole Whole Half Whole Whole Whole Half
Fifty percent of all rock and roll songs
Of the fifties
Had the same melody
Here are the chords
One six-minor four five
My all time favorite rock and roll song
Why Must I Be A Teenager In Love
One six-minor four five

Letter From An Old Man

I am writing this letter in response to your letter
I believe it to be an inquiry about something I said or did
If you did not write me a letter that required a response
Please discard this
Some of the memories I have of days past are mine
And some may be the memories of others
Some were incidental and some were conversational
If the incident left no scars as a reminder
It is possible they were conversation and misunderstood
If you do not receive this response
You will know I forgot to mail it

Life and Justice

The young soldier was from West Virginia
He had a scar on his cheek where his father had hit him
The young man would not follow orders
He said
My father told me to never say sir to no man
I had him thrown in the brig for a few days
I visited him one day to see if he had improved
I asked
What are you doing in the army anyway
He says
I joined when my father went to prison
They sent him up for something he didn't do
I said
Do you find it ironic
That you're in the brig for the same reason

Me As A Critic

I propose that the phrase
Words cannot express
Should be banned from letters of condolence
Having disqualified
The whole of the English language
As a means of expressing oneself
Further efforts are futile

Limo Logic

Logic drives me crazy
My limo driver was cursed with it
One day we pull up to a stop sign
I look to my right up a one-way street
I say
There's the studio but we can't go that way
It's a one-way street
He says
We can go that way
I say
It's a one-way street
He says
We can go that way
I often think about that
We had a gas pedal and a steering wheel
He was right

Long Arm Of The Law

My maternal grandfather was county judge
My father was temporarily out of work
The judge called the county sheriff
Give my son-in-law a job as deputy
Yes sir
Two in the morning
There is a local drunk outside
He is yelling
Come and get me Deputy Hall
Come and get me Deputy Hall
My father gets dressed
Quietly circles around behind the drunk
Grabs him by the arm and says
I got you
The drunk fainted

Lost and Found

We pulled into the parking lot in Las Vegas
Been on the road for a couple weeks
Had a lot of cash in the bus safe
We rented a safe deposit box at the casino
One day I decided to gamble a bit
I went to the safe deposit box room
The guard opened the door of the room for me
I walked through the aisle looking for my number
There on the stainless steel counter in the room
Was a banded bundle of Canadian money
I picked it up and stuck it in my jacket pocket
Five-thousand Canadian dollars
I am a terrible crook
For thirty years I have been trying to remember
Where in the hell I hid that money

Marty Robbins

Sitting in the lobby of a hotel in Dallas
Three in the morning
My road manager was putting my things in my room
He would bring me a key when finished
Marty Robbins walked in through the revolving door
He was dressed in stage clothes
He had been to L.A. to pick up some new threads
Tailor-made by Nudie
I stood up and spoke to him
I said
Man you look great
How in the world did you lose all that weight
He said
I had a heart attack

Maybe She-Maybe We

Leaving Germany after two and a half years
A duffel bag and an army uniform
I sat by the window in a train on a cool rainy day
A woman was standing on the platform outside
She was wearing a pale blue dress
And a well-tailored trench coat
Tears in her eyes
She raised her hand to wave goodbye
Blonde hair and blue eyes crying in the rain
I looked to see if she could be waving at someone else
Few people in the car and none noticed her
I don't think I knew her
I waved back to her and she waved again
Crying more now
Maybe I had known her
Maybe she came down and waved goodbye to all soldiers
Maybe she...
Maybe we...
Maybe she...
The train started moving
I'll never know

Me As An Artist

I paint
With small brushes on canvas
Don't let this frighten you
There are no pictures in this little book
At least none of my paintings
I have hired tutors to teach me
Read dozens of books
Fascinated with art
What is this
Landscapes with no people
The way the planet was before we got here
And architecture
People who paint buildings should use those big five gallon
buckets
And have ladders
I like to paint portraits
People's faces
God has made millions and millions of people
And none of them look exactly alike
Why did God mix up the mechanics of our DNA with that of
snowflakes

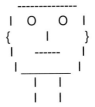

My Father's Church

The church was built on a wide place in the road
Between Carter City and Olive Hill Kentucky
Twelve miles apart
I never knew the origin of the one-room building
The church was white with a wooden cross on top
Saturday nights
Young people would park and party there
In summer they would make love between the gravestones
I considered it a place of cosmic irony
People coming and going
Sunday mornings before Sunday school and church
I had the unenviable job of cleaning up the area
Beer cans and whiskey bottles
Condoms cigarette butts candy wrappers and panties
My father the preacher never complained
He said this may be as close to a church as they ever get

No Offense

I never consorted with prostitutes
No offense
I was in the military for eight years
They camped around our bases
They walked the streets
With me it was not where they were
It was where they had been
Old prostitutes work for less
Like old singers and actors
Old lawyers charge more
The only comparable profession where experience counts
I asked a preacher friend about prostitution
He said they were just trying to make a living
It's a Jesus thing you know
The woman at the well
Cast the first stone
No offense

Pitfall

Perth Australia
Casino gig
Phone rings in my room
Yes
Ready for sound check
Be there
Downstairs I walk into theater
It is dark
Only the stage is lighted
I can see the band
I am walking in pitch darkness
Feeling my way along
The lights come on
I am one step away from falling
Into the orchestra pit
Twenty feet down
Full of metal chairs
Newspaper story
ENTERTAINER KILLED
BY BEAST HE TAMED

Road Hog Or Die

Thirty-four years
Eight hours a day
Four days a week
Do the math
That's how many hours
I spent looking out the window
Of a country music tour bus
If I am reincarnated
As a country music picker
While I am still in the crib
Shoot me
Please

Saint Louis Blues

On my tour bus
Traveling west into the sunset
My fiddle player is riding shotgun
Sipping from a bottle of whiskey
He stands up and turns to me
Tom T. I hate to see it
I looked into his watery eyes
See what
He sings
That evening sun go down

Say What

Sitting in the White House
At the foot of Lincoln's bed
In front of me is a copy of The Gettysburg Address
In Lincoln's handwriting
President Jimmy Carter is relaxing in a chair
Towel around his neck from his morning run
I say
Mister President this is a great day in the life of a country boy
The President says
Are you talking about me

Song Police

Phone rings
We found a song of yours we like
We want to change a few words and record it
I say
I like it the way I wrote it
Record something else
And now we meet the song police
In a board room listening
They are considering politics
Demographics
Video possibilities
Will it offend
Will it make people stop and think
Can't have that
Can you dance to it
Is it too long
Too short
Is it enough like the last hit we heard
Songs on trial

Songs I Never Published
(1)

I shot the red nosed reindeer
You should have seen him fall
I shot the red nosed reindeer
His head is on my wall
I shot the red nosed reindeer
Little kids cried all day
I shot the red nosed reindeer
God bless the NRA

Star Power

Richard and his wife called for a meeting with me
In my office
Richard was a young singer
He sang two songs before I came on
It gave the sound man
A chance to get the bugs out of the sound system
Before my performance
They came in and sat down
His wife said
You know and we know
That most of the people who come to your shows
Are really there to see Richard
You can tell by the applause
We think Richard should have his own career
I said
That being the case I think so too
I don't know what happened to Richard and his wife

Sweating The Small Stuff

He was a drummer in my band
We stopped at a lot of diners
He would order his food
After the waitress had brought it
He would stand up and start yelling
Bring me a glass of milk
Bring me a glass of milk
It took three weeks for me to tire
One day I decided to ask about it
Why not order milk to start with
It gets warm while they cook the food
I like my milk ice-cold
Back on the tour bus
I pulled my road manager aside
Fire that son-of-a-bitch

The Cold Shoulder

Our tour in Alaska
Land of the midnight sun
Outside it's forty below zero
Inside a honky-tonk
The days are fifteen minutes long
Sunrise at 11:15 sunset at 11:30
P.M. A.M. I never knew
A person comes to my table
Dressed in fur and leather boots
With rawhide leggings
Inside a parka hood
All I can see is a nose and black eyes
Do you want to dance
I look closely
Who's in there

The Day I Found Out I Was Old

I pulled up to the window at McDonald's
A very young lady said
Your order please
Egg McMuffin French Fries and a Coke
She returned
Sir we only have one kind of fries

Rabbits and Songwriters

People from all over the world
From all walks of life
Come to Nashville - Music City
Believing in music
The way children believe in magic
Most do not make it and go home
Others
Not accepting failure
Live under bridges
Where they laugh at people
Who do not believe
That rabbits live in hats

Tour Bus Anger Management

My fiddle player was named Robert
He weighed one-hundred fifteen pounds
Shy and scholarly
My steel player was named Bob
He weighed two-hundred and twenty-five
Played football
My fiddle player knocked on my state-room door
Come in
He stood there for a moment
Biting his lip
He asked
What would happen if Bob and I had a fight
He'd kill you
He bit his lip and said
That's what I was thinking

Why I Loved The Army

In the late fifties you could join the army
And they would promise your place of duty
Private Carpenter chose Germany
Two years and eight months later
In Germany
He came to me
I was his immediate superior
He says
I will be going home in a few weeks
I want to marry a German woman
And take her back with me
He wants me to meet her
We go to a small German cafe'
She walks in
She is in her mid forties
Worn looking and has a limp
Carpenter is twenty-one and handsome
He asks me to please sign the consent
The paperwork would go to battalion to regiment
Army chain of command
He said I love this woman trust me
I signed and it went through at the top
A few days before he left he told me
His father served in Germany during the war
Fathered a son
Carpenter came to Germany to marry his mother
And take her home
The United States Army paid for everything

Why I Quit Working Vegas

Las Vegas lights up backs up against the desert
And takes on the whole world
I would take my band there for weeks at a time
They lost rent utilities mortgage alimony and all
On the bus leaving Vegas
I would go to the safe on the bus
And get a stack of hundred-dollar bills
How much did you lose Bill
750
How 'bout you Fred
1500
And so on
How 'bout you Poco
Don't worry 'bout it T
I'm just gonna shoot myself

Why Songwriter

The irony abounds
My ashes in the ground
Which trod the earth and made songs
Look
I am still moving
The universe expanding and speeding up
And me with it
To what end I do not know
Unless I am the reason for it all
Which is a laughable thought
But who knows

Yes Jesus Likes Me

We are all characters in a Bible
To be written later
As we go through life
Although we have been told The Story
Hundreds of times
We cannot resist the urge to look around
And think
Thinking is sinful
So we must be careful
The word *love* is tossed around a lot
I don't care much for being loved
I like to be liked
Love introduces a lot of threatening possibilities
I invented my own religion
God likes me

Apology

To be honest
The only poems that come to mind
If I consider poetry
Mary had a little lamb
Jack and Jill went up the hill
Humpty Dumpty
Classic stuff for the ages
Everything else is something else
My friends had to read this stuff
That's not what friends are for
Heard a story one time
Old poet sat by his fireplace
Wrote one great poem after another
And as he finished them
Dropped them into the fire
I have a fireplace
But I didn't do that